Maritime
ABC

an alphabet from Canada

written and illustrated by
J.R. Mason-Browne

FOUR
EAST
PUBLICATIONS

To Ju... 2013

*Happy reading
Missy, Mike
and
Juno!
♡
Auntie Jo*

When I was in the Maritimes

I saw an...

Aa

Apple in Annapolis Valley,
Nova Scotia

Bb

Boat on Brackley Beach,
Prince Edward Island

Cc

Cat in Charlottetown,
Prince Edward Island

Dd

Dog in Donkin,
Cape Breton, Nova Scotia

Ee

Eagle in Edmundston,
New Brunswick

Ff

Fiddle in Fredericton,
New Brunswick

Gg

Girl at Green Gables,
Prince Edward Island

Hh

House in Halifax,
Nova Scotia

Ii

Island near Ingonish,
Cape Breton, Nova Scotia

Jj

Jam in Joggins, Nova Scotia

Kk

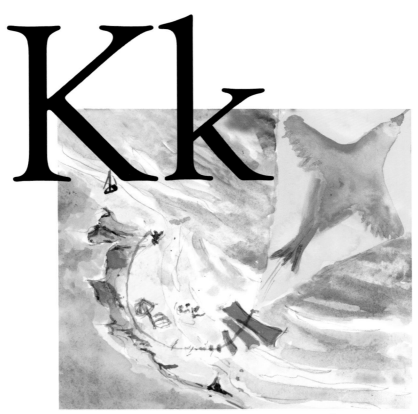

Kite over Kingsboro,
Prince Edward Island

Ll

Lighthouse in Louisbourg,
Nova Scotia

Mm

Mouse in Miramichi,
New Brunswick

Nn

Nut in Neils Harbour,
Cape Breton, Nova Scotia

Oo

Owl in Oromocto,
New Brunswick

Pp

Piper playing at
Peggy's Cove, N.S.

Qq

Queen in Queensland,
Nova Scotia

Rr

Rabbit in Rustico,
Prince Edward Island

Ss

Seagull in Sydney,
Cape Breton, Nova Scotia

Tt

Train in Truro,
Nova Scotia

Uu

Umbrella
over
Urbania,
Nova Scotia

Vv

Van in Victoria,
Prince Edward Island

Ww

Whale near
Whipple Point, N.S.

Xx

Xylophone on Xanadu Drive,
Antigonish County, Nova Scotia

Yy

Yacht near Yarmouth,
Nova Scotia

Zodiac on Zwicker Lake,
Nova Scotia

Wow!
Look at all the people I met,
and the things I saw
in the Maritimes!

Aa

Bb

Cc

Dd

Ee

Ff

Gg

Hh

Ii

Jj

Kk

Ll

Mm

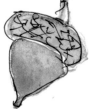

Nn

Oo Pp Qq Rr

Ss Tt Uu Vv

Ww Xx Yy Zz

For family and friends
who have given me unending encouragement.

Third printing April 2012
editing by Grayce Rogers

text and cover layout and design by J.R. Mason-Browne

Printed and bound in Canada

This is a work of fiction.
Any resemblance to actual events or persons, living or dead, is purely coincidental.

Published in Canada by Four East Publications
P.O. Box 3087 Tantallon, Nova Scotia B3Z 4G9
www.glenmargaret.com

Library and Archives Canada Cataloguing in Publication

Mason-Browne, Jane, 1958-
Maritime ABC / J.R. Mason-Browne.

ISBN 978-1-897462-10-2

1. English language--Alphabet--Juvenile literature. 2. Alphabet books.
3. Maritime Provinces--Pictorial works--Juvenile literature. I. Title.

PE1155.M383 2009 j421'.1 C2009-902504-3